TABLE O

1 INTRODUCTION TO THE DAY CARE BUSINESS 5
   THERE IS HIGH DEMAND FOR GOOD DAY CARE 6

2 GETTING STARTED 8
   EDUCATION MATTERS 8
     If one does not have an education degree 8
     THE NEED FOR A business plan 10
   FRANCHISING AND RUNNING A DAY CARE FROM OUTSIDE THE HOME 10

3 LOCATION, LOCATION, LOCATION 13
   HOME BASED DAY CARES 13
   OPERATING AN OUT-OF-HOME DAY CARE 14
     Finding a Location 15
     Other facility ideas 17

4 BUSINESS BASICS 18
   WHO TO SERVE? 18
   SAFETY 18
   HOURS 19
   STAFFING 20
   FOOD 21
   LICENSING 22
     Day care Licensing Requirements By State 22
   ACTIVITIES 42
   INSURANCE 43
     Choosing an Insurance company 44

5 MARKETING 46
- THE SIGN 46
- BROCHURE 46
- GRAND OPENING OPEN HOUSE 47
- LOCAL MEDIA 48

6 CUSTOMER SERVICE 49

7 BEING PROFITABLE 52
- UPFRONT EXPENSES 52
- ONGOING EXPENSES 53
- TUITION RATES 54
- SETTING THE DAY CARE APART 55

8 WHY DAY CARES FAIL 56
- FINANCIAL FAILURE 56
- FAILURE TO ADHERE TO LEGAL GUIDELINES 57
- FAILURE TO SATISFY CUSTOMERS 57

9 CREATING A LONG TERM PLAN 59

CONCLUSION 62

ABOUT THE AUTHOR 63

How to Start A Profitable Day care Business From Home

*DEDICATED TO MY GRANDMOTHERS, LULA
AND BEATRICE, FOR SETTING FINE EXAMPLES
AND SHOWING UNCONDITIONAL LOVE*

1
INTRODUCTION TO THE DAY CARE BUSINESS

The day care industry is thriving. In fact, this is one industry that the recent economic downturn has been very kind to. More stay-at-home moms have entered the workplace to help make ends meet, so more children have entered day care than ever before. Running a day care can be a smart career choice, because it is a business that will always be in demand. In fact, in areas where there are few day cares, many day cares have a waiting list for openings. This does not mean, however, that running a day care is easy, nor does it mean the day care provider will immediately be making millions from the business. There are numerous hurdles to overcome in order to make a day care business successful and profitable. The day care provider will need to learn ways to keep costs to a minimum while still providing excellent services.

There are wonderful rewards to being a day care owner. Not only can a mother work from home and be available for their children, but also it offers the opportunity to pursue other interests, such as obtaining an education, while still running business. With hard work, running a day care can assist in facilitating many personal goals.

THERE IS HIGH DEMAND FOR GOOD DAY CARE

Experts predict that the demand for day care centers will continue to increase. This is fueled by the fact that today's mothers were likely in day care themselves as children. Therefore, they may have very fond memories of the experience and feel comfortable leaving their children in day care centers, assuming they are convinced their children's needs are being appropriately met.

Gone are the days when new mothers left their children in the hands of Grandma while they went to work. Today, it is likely that Grandma is working as well. While today's mothers are comfortable with the day care setting, these mothers are also better educated than mothers in the past, so their expectations are higher.

Today's mothers realize that the most important years of a child's development are the years between the ages one and six. These mothers are not looking for a babysitter; they are looking for an age-appropriate educational experience in a loving and nurturing environment. They can likely find a babysitter at a lower cost than a day care,, but they are forgoing the less expensive option for one that gives their children a better educational and emotional start.

If one plans to be a day care provider, one must demonstrate to potential clients that the day care provider understands the needs of young children and has the experience, education and staffing to meet those needs. When talking about taking care of people's *children* – one must understand that the parents will expect a lot from the day care provider and that they will not tolerate care below the standard they expect. If one provides excellent care and stimulation for the children, the parents will value the service immensely. If one does not meet those needs, the parent will most likely move their children to another facility immediately. This will lead to bad reviews of the service, and there is great power in word of mouth.

This book will provide assistance for getting started on the road to running a successful day care. The book will explain the correct path regarding licensing requirements and also offer tips on how to run a business in a way that is profitable and successful. For those people whom love children, running a day care can be a very rewarding experience. But, regardless how much one loves children, it must be understood that it is a business, and must be treated as such in order for it to be successful and profitable.

2
GETTING STARTED

EDUCATION MATTERS

It was noted earlier that today's parents are more educated than previous generations and have higher expectations of child care providers. One expectation is the day care center will have the appropriate credentials to run the business. In most cases this means, at the very least, the day care provider has the required certification in childhood development. A master's degree is preferable, but many people have been quite successful with a bachelor's degree or certification such as a The Child Development Associate Credential, particularly when it is paired with years of experience.

IF ONE DOES NOT HAVE AN EDUCATION DEGREE

Many people decide to run a day care center because they realize what a profitable business it can be, not because they have a background in child development and a love for children.

One can certainly be successful as the owner of a day care center without being a child development expert, but it is critical to acknowledge the skills needed and make up for any shortcoming. Few parents will accept child care provided by a day care where the principal operator has no child development education or experience. If one wants to earn top dollar for the services, simply having raised one's own children will not be enough. There are several ways to make up for what may be lacking in one's credentials.

The simplest are:

- **Find a partner**
  Some of the most successful day cares are owned by a team - one partner with the business experience required to make the business profitable and the other with the child development experience required to come up with effective programs and policies for the business. It is a great way to build a one-of-a kind program that will attract well-educated clients.

- **Learning is the greatest investment**
  Even if one does not pursue a child development degree, an indivdual can enhance one's knowledge of running a day care by taking classes designed for day care operators. There are even online classes one can take designed to teach how to create appropriate child care classes. If one decides to take this path, it may take some time to get the business up and running. It may still be wise to hire an accredited teacher to work on curriculum development to enhance the credentials of the child care center.

- **Hire a director**
  If one does not want a business partner, and does not want to take the time to earn a child development degree, one can hire a day care director who has the education and experience needed to create the programs and train the staff. Many large companies that own day care chains employ this method and hire a director to administer the child care programs according to the corporate policy.

THE NEED FOR A BUSINESS PLAN

Regardless of whether the center is a sole proprietorship or a partnership, a business plan is a necessity. Not only will a business plan help outline the business in detail, but it will also be a requirement for bank loans and potential investors..

Writing a business plan is not an impossible task, but writing a quality plan can be challenging. The Small Business Administration is a government organization that helps small business owners. SCORE is a division of this agency, and offers counseling on a multitude of issues regarding starting and running a business. Their business plan template is easy to follow and can help one create a professional business plan. For the template and more small business help, visit SCORE and take the online business plan writing class.

FRANCHISING AND RUNNING A DAY CARE FROM OUTSIDE THE HOME

Another option for starting a day care is to invest in a franchise. There are many franchise options available. Franchising can simplify the process of starting a day care center.

Here are some advantages to franchising:

- **Name recognition**
  If one franchises with a well known day care center company, the day care center gains instant name recognition, and may have an advatage with parents who have used this day care franchise at another location.

- **Business in a box**
  With a franchise, all the information needed to start the business is provided: parameters for location, programs for the curriculum, and amount and types of staff members to hire. Occasionally, menus for meals are provided. All that remains to do is hire the staff and follow the programs and policies. If one buys into a successful franchise, one should have a recipe for success.

There are also some disadvantages to being a franchisee. In fact, some of the advantages can also be disadvantages.

These include:

- **Name recognition**
  Just as one may gain some clients because they previously had good experiences with day care centers under the chosen franchise, the center may also lose potential clients because they had unpleasant experiences with the chosen franchise. It is important to choose a franchise wisely and to investigate any other day cares in the area operating under the same franchise. If the franchise had a lot of complaints, it may reflect poorly on the new franchise with the same name. In addition, some parents will eschew franchise day cares, because they prefer a smaller, more personal environment for their children.

- **Business in a box**
  Though a franchise will provide all the tools necessary to start the business, the franchise will also expect all their policies and programs be followed. There is also less opportunity to be creative and unique with a franchise. In many ways, the franchise business owner both works for one's own day care center and also works for the franchise.

- **Upfront cash**
  Many franchises require a substantial upfront cash investment. The cost of opening an independent day care center must be compared to the cost of buying into a franchise.

In addition to buying a franchise directly from the corporate headquarters, an existing franchise day care may be up for sale. In this case, the center is simply taken over by the new owner and the center already has clients in place. Before purchase, the existing franchise day care must be investigated to make sure it is in good standing with the franchise. The existing center must be profitable and reputable in order for it to be desirable to purchase.

For more information on day care franchising, visit Hoovers or Franchise Opportunities.

3
LOCATION, LOCATION, LOCATION

One of the first decisions to be made about opening a day care center is the location. If the budget is low, a small, in-home day care is a good option. However, this solution is not feasible for all situations, and often a franchise day care will require an out-of-home location be utilized.

HOME BASED DAY CARES

There are advantages and disadvantages to both in-home and out-of-home day cares.

These are some of the pros to running a day care center in one's home:

- **Faster time to get going**
  The set up and preparation for opening a home day care can be accomplished within a few weeks or months, depending on the state in which it is located. If the day care is to be opened in a separate location, there are more steps to complete, such as finding a location and making that location suitable.

- **Smaller out of pocket expenses**
  In-home day care centers can be set up for far less money than at a separate location. In large part,

the amount saved in rent or lease payments may make it possible to set up a new day care without a loan.

- **Tax advantages**
  There are many tax advantages to operating a day care at home, including the ability to deduct a portion of the rent or mortgage, utility payments, and property taxes as a business expense. One should consult with a tax advisor to help determine the tax advantages.

- **Lower overhead**
  There are far fewer overhead costs running an in-home day care. For example, food costs can be offset by the Federal Food Program, which will save money. The main costs will be supplies, food, beverages, insurance, and advertising.

OPERATING AN OUT-OF-HOME DAY CARE

Just as there are advantages to a home-based day care, there are advantages to running an out-of-home day care center.

Consider the following advantages to having a separate facility.

- **The ability to care for more children**
  A separate facility often allows for more space for more children, which should make it easier to be profitable. Each state has restrictions on the amount of children allowed in a home day care setting.

- **Business is kept separate from home**
  One may have difficulty separating work from

home when working from home. This can be minimized if the home day care is located in a completely separate area from the main living quarters, such as a finished basement that can be solely devoted to the day care. In addition, parents may be more likely to ask that their children be kept longer hours when the day care is in one's home.

- **Out-of-home day cares are more likely to qualify for a grant**
  Most grants disqualify home based day cares, because they do not serve enough children in a home environment. So, if grant money is needed to help start the business, a separate facility should be considered.

- **A separate day care facility Is a real asset that is sellable**
  Eventually, one will most likely want to get out of the child care business. A separate facility and business is an asset that can be sold when the time comes. This is not an option when running an in-home day care.

FINDING A LOCATION

If the decision is to open a day care in a separate location, the search for the facility must happen well in advance. The business plan should include an idea of how many children to serve, and how much capital is needed for startup costs. Monthly expenses (i.e., rent or mortgage, supplies, etc.) should also be included in the business plan. It is critical to know these important numbers before searching for a viable facility .

The number of children served and the local regulations will designate the amount of square footage needed. The amount of startup capital determines how much remodeling can be done, and the monthly budgeted rent or mortgage amount will help narrow down which buildings are feasible. The budgeted numbers may need to be adjusted if finding a feasible facility is not in the planned budget parameters.

In a perfect world, these are the attributes of a profitable location for your day care.

- A location where there's a defined need (no other nearby day care, or not enough nearby day care to serve the population)

- A location on a main thoroughfare and set back from the street

- A location on the right-hand side of the street as you head into the business district.

- A covered drive up by the front door for drop off

- Ample parking

The idea is to make drop off and pick up as easy as possible. Most parents prefer the day care be located closer to their home than to work, because this makes it more convenient to take their children to day care on days they are not be working. In addition, it is beneficial for children to avoid a long commute.

Making drop off and pick up easy and quick is essential. With a covered drive up at the door, parents can drop off their children with just a few steps inside the door and without having to turn off the car. On rainy days, babies do not get wet.

Once inside, the facility should have a lobby, be equipped with a commercial kitchen, have an area that can be used for dining, and have classrooms. Preferably, some of the classrooms would be equipped with bathrooms.

For the outdoor space, a fenced-in playground is desirable. If the outdoor area is large; adding playground equipment and a fence should not be too difficult or costly.

OTHER FACILITY IDEAS

While a retail building or a building that has previously been used as a day care are great choices, there are some other types of buildings worth considering. While these may not initially seem ideal, they may offer lower rent, which will make them easier (and less expensive) to customize.

- **Churches**
  Churches are a good choice for a day care facility. They likely already have classrooms (for Sunday School), a kitchen, good parking and good drop off. The opportunity to recruit clients through the church is also advantageous.

- **Houses**
  Renting a house with a good sized back yard may also be an option. A small amount of remodeling can often turn a ranch style house into a great small day care facility.

4
BUSINESS BASICS

Once a business plan is created, a location is secured, the amount of children served is decided, it is time to make some very basic, yet important, decisions about the operation of the business.

Here are things to consider:

WHO TO SERVE?

First, a target audience needs to be identified. One needs to determine the age and education level of the children one will serve. Also, the days and hours of operation of the day care need to be established. Once these decisions are made, one can move forward with the operation of the day care.

SAFETY

Safety procedures need to be determined before a day care can open. Prospective employees should be screened with background checks. A locking system needs to be determined. The front entrance must be staffed to prevent any strangers from entering the day care. All of these steps will keep the children safe and give the parents peace of mind.

- All doors should stay locked during business hours, so that children can not leave unattended. Cameras should be placed in each room so that all teachers are subject to supervision at all times. Some day care centers give parents access to web cams to observe the children and staff.

- Play areas must be fenced, and gates must be locked to keep children in. Play areas must always be supervised.

- Fire safety is critical, particularly in a facility where doors are locked from the inside during the day. Of course, the building will need to pass inspection by the fire marshal, but the marshal can also help implement a fire safety program and ensure that all employees are properly trained.

- Food safety is critical. Some children have food allergies, which can sometimes be life threatening. The staff must be responsible for keeping these allergies posted and for ensuring that allergic children are not served foods to which they could have a reaction.

- Food safety also means good sanitation practices, particularly in the kitchen. A kitchen staff employee should be certified in food safety, so that food is prepared properly and only safe, fresh ingredients are used..

HOURS

Most day care centers are open from 6:00 am until 6:00 pm Monday through Friday. These business hours work well for most situations, but there are reasons why alternate hours should be considered.

- **Big cities with heavy traffic**
In many large cities where traffic is very heavy and parents may have a long commute, day cares stay open later than 6:00 pm. For example, in suburban Atlanta, every day care is open until 6:30 pm and some are open until 7:00 pm.

- **A lot of shift work in the area**
If a lot of parents in the local area work for one particular company that has work hours outside the normal 8:00-5:00 standard, alternate hours should be considered to accommodate those parents. For instance, many plants have shifts that begin at 6:00 am. To accommodate those parents, day cares would have to open by 5:30 am.

STAFFING

This particular business item might seem like one of the most difficult business decisions, but in truth, it is probably simpler than one imagines. Because the law dictates the qualifications of the staff, it is easy to follow the guidelines provided. There is a specific ratio of staff to student that the day care must follow.

Keep in mind that early in the morning and late in the day, when children are trickling in and out, the center may be able to operate with fewer staff members by combining classrooms during these times. This helps to stagger staff shifts.

The teacher to student ratios typically only apply to the staff actually working in the classrooms with the children. But, in addition to these employees, one needs to consider the following staffing requirements:

- Kitchen staff – lunches are typically provided by the day care, and at times, breakfast as well.

- Reception staff
- Custodial staff

FOOD

Important food decisions must also be made. A day care is expected to serve a hot lunch each day, and many parents also appreciate the option for a breakfast. If breakfast is also added, the day care can charge an additional $8 - $12 for weekly tuition. Snacks should also be provided by the day care. Most day care centers enroll in the Child and Adult Care Food Program (cacfp), which provides reimbursement for the meals and snacks provided to the children enrolled in the facility.

It is a wise idea to hire a nutritionist or dietician to prepare the menus and provide recipes. They can be hired as a consultant and they will prepare several weeks of menus, including providing nutritional information on each recipe. With a month's worth of menus prepared, the day care can simply rotate these without needing new menus for months. The center will learn which meals the children enjoy and which ones they do not like. The unpopular menu items should be substituted to meet the needs of the children.

Once the menus and recipes are prepared, a cook is needed to prepare the food. Breakfast can either be homemade food, or simple prepared foods like cereal and fruit. With a little extra time in the kitchen, the cook can put together snacks such as cut up fruit and veggies for after lunch. The remainder of the snacks can be ready-to-go foods like pretzels and crackers.

One of the biggest opportunities for cutting costs is in the kitchen, but nutrition and taste cannot be sacrificed. It is important to buy food in bulk and to take advantage of good deals when they arise. One should start looking for a food vendor before opening the facility, so there is time to negotiate prices and to shop around. A nutritionist can come up with meals that kids love but that are inexpensive to prepare and are healthy for the children.

LICENSING

Licensing is critical; one cannot do business without it. An owner should determine the licensing requirements for the state before putting the business plan together. Every state is different, and the center must follow the state's licensing requirements exactly.

This is a list of the licensing agencies state by state, with contact information for each:

DAY CARE LICENSING REQUIREMENTS BY STATE

- **Starting a day care in Alabama**
    - Department of Human Resources
      Child Care Services Division
      Gordon Persons Building
      50 North Ripley Street
      Montgomery, AL 36130
      Phone: 334-242-1425
      Fax: 334-353-1491
      Website:
      http://www.dhr.state.al.us/page.asp?pageid=648
      Requirements:
      http://www.dhr.state.al.us/page.asp?pageid=267

- **Starting a day care in Alaska**
    - Department of Health & Social Services
      Division of Public Assistance

Child Care Program Office
619 E. Ship Creek Ave., Suite 230
Anchorage, AK 99501-2341
Phone: 907- 269-4500
Hotline: 888-268-4632 (within state)
Fax: 907-269-1064
Website: http://health.hss.state.ak.us/dpa/programs/ccare/
Requirements: http://health.hss.state.ak.us/dpa/programs/ccare/regs.html

- **Starting a day care in Arizona**

    o Arizona Department of Health Services
    Department of Licensure
    150 N 18th Avenue, Suite 400
    Phoenix, AZ 85007
    Phone: 602-364-2539
    Hotline: 800-615-8555
    Fax: 602-364-4768

    Website: http://www.azdhs.gov/als/childcare/index.htm
    Requirements: http://www.azdhs.gov/als/childcare/cc_apps.htm

- **Starting a day care in Arkansas**

    o Arkansas Department of Human Services
    Division of Child Care and Early Childhood Education
    Child Care Licensing
    Unit 700 Main Street
    P.O. Box 1437, Slot 720
    Little Rock, AR 72203-1437
    Phone: 501-682-8590
    Hotline: 800-445-3316
    Fax: 501-682-2317
    Website: http://www.state.ar.us/child_care/

Requirements: http://www.state.ar.us/child care/provider.html

- **Starting a day care in California**

  o Department of Social Services
    Community Care Licensing Division
    Child Care Program
    744 P Street, Mail Stop 19-48
    Sacramento, CA 95814
    Phone: 916-229-4500
    Fax: 916-229-4508
    Website: http://ccl.dss.cahwnet.gov/PG487.htm
    County Requirements:
    http://ccl.dss.cahwnet.gov/res/pdf/cclistingMaster.pdf

- **Starting a day care in Colorado**

  o Department of Human Services
    Division of Child Care
    1575 Sherman Street, First Floor
    Denver, CO 80203-1714
    Phone: 303-866-5958 or 800-799-5876
    Fax: 303-866-4453
    Website: http://www.state.co.us/oed/industry-license/IndDetail.cfm?id=27
    Requirements: http://www.denvergov.org/Business_Licensing/template14846.asp

- **Starting a ay care in Connecticut**

  o CT Department of Public Health
    Child Day Care Licensing
    410 Capitol Avenue
    Mail Station 12 DAC
    P.O. Box 340308
    Hartford, CT 06134-0308
    Phone: 860-509-8045
    Fax: 860-509-7541
    Website:
    http://www.dph.state.ct.us/BRS/Day_Care/day_care.htm

Requirements: http://www.ct-clic.com/detail.asp?code=1851
http://www.ct-clic.com/detail.asp?code=1849

- **Starting a day care in Delaware**

    o Delaware Department of Children, Youth and Their Families
    Office of Child Care Licensing
    1825 Faulkland Road
    Wilmington, DE 19805-1121
    Phone: 302-892-5800
    Fax: 302-633-5112
    Website: http://www.state.de.us/kids/occl.htm
    Requirements: http://www.state.de.us/kids/occl/occl_resources.shtml

- **Starting a day care in District of Columbia**

    o District of Columbia Health Regulation Administration
    Child and Residential Care Facility Division
    825 N. Capitol St., NE. 2nd Floor
    Washington, DC 20002
    Phone: 202-442-5888
    Fax: 202-442-9430
    Website: http://www.dhs.dc.gov/dhs/cwp/view,a,3,Q,622842,dhsNav,|34074|.asp
    Requirements: http://mblr.dc.gov/information/bbl/index.asp

- **Starting a day care in Florida**

    o Department of Children & Families
    Child Care Regulation Office
    1317 Winewood Blvd. Building 6 Room 389A
    Tallahassee, FL 32399-0700
    Phone: 850-488-4900
    Fax: 850-488-9584

Website: http://www.myflorida.com/child care/
Requirements: http://www.dcf.state.fl.us/child care/licensing.shtml

- **Starting a day care in Georgia**

  o Bright From the Start: Georgia Department of Early Care and Learning
  10 Park Place South, Suite 200
  Atlanta, GA 30303
  Phone: 404-651-7182
  Fax: 404-657-8936
  Hotline: 888-4GA-PREK
  Website: http://ors.dhr.georgia.gov/portal/site/DHR-ORS/menuitem.a7e86d3fa49a7a608e738510da1010a0/?vgnextoid=7cc344c26e5fff00VgnVCM100000bf01010aRCRD
  Requirements: http://www.nccic.org/statedata/statepro/georgia.html#licensing

- **Starting a day care in Hawaii**

  o Hawaii Department of Human Services
  Benefit, Employment & Support Services Division
  820 Mililani Street, Suite 606
  Honolulu, HI 96813-2936
  Phone: 808-586-7050
  Fax: 808-586-5229
  Website: http://www.hawaii.gov/dhs/dhs/self-sufficiency/child care
  Requirements: http://www.hawaii.gov/dhs/self-sufficiency/child care/licensing/

- **Starting a day care in Idaho**

  o Idaho Department of Health & Welfare
  Bureau of Family & Community Services
  450 W. State Street
  Boise, ID 83720-0036

Hotline: (2-1-1 Idaho CareLine) Dial 2-1-1 or 800-926-2588; (TDD) 208-332-7205
Phone: Dial 2-1-1 (within state) or 800-926-2588 (nationwide)
Fax: 208-334-5531
Website: http://www.healthandwelfare.idaho.gov/portal/alias__Rainbow/lang__en-US/tabID__3374/DesktopDefault.aspx
Requirements: Licensing Requirements for Starting a Day care in Idaho

- **Starting a day care in Illinois**

    o Department of Children & Family Services
    Office of Licensing
    406 E. Monroe Street, Station 60
    Springfield, IL 62701-1498
    Phone: 217-785-2688 ; 877-746-0829
    Fax: 217-524-3347
    Website: http://www.state.il.us/dcfs/daycare/index.shtml
    http://www.dhs.state.il.us/ts/ccfs/ccd/indexbackup10-28-03.asp
    Requirements: Licensing Requirements for Starting a Day care in Illinois

- **Starting a day care in Indiana**

    IN Family & Social Services Administration
    Division of Family and Children
    Bureau of Child Development - Licensing Section
    402 W. Washington Street, Room W-386
    Indianapolis, IN 46204

    o For center-based child-care call: 317-232-4469
    For Family Child Care call: 317-232-4521 or 317-234-2100
    For ministries call: Phone: 317-233-5414
    Fax: 317-234-1513

Website: http://www.in.gov/fssa/carefinder/learnmore/
Requirements
http://www.in.gov/fssa/carefinder/become/

- **Starting a day care in Iowa**

    o for center-based child care
    Iowa Department of Human Services
    Division of Behavioral Development &
    Protective Services
    Child Care Unit
    Hoover State Office Building 5th Floor
    Des Moines, IA 50319-0114
    Phone: 515-281-5584

    o for Family Child Care
    Department of Human Services
    Division of Behavioral Development &
    Protective Services
    Child Care Unit
    Hoover State Office Building, 5th Floor
    Des Moines, IA 50319
    Phone: 515-281-5584
    Fax: 515-242-6036

    Website: http://www.dhs.iowa.gov/Consumers/Child_Care/Child careMenu.html

    o Requirements:
    http://www.dhs.state.ia.us/children_family/child_care/index.html

- **Starting a day care in Kansas**

    o Department of Health and Environment
    Bureau of Child Care Licensing & Regulation
    Curtis State Office Bldg
    1000 SW Jackson, Suite 200
    Topeka, KS 66612-1274
    Phone: 785-296-1270

Fax: 785-296-0803
Website: http://www.kdheks.gov/bcclr/regs/day care_groupday care_regs.html
Requirements: http://www.kdheks.gov/bcclr/lic_and_reg.html

- **Starting a day care in Kentucky**

    o Kentucky Cabinet for Health and Family Services
    Division of Regulated Child Care
    Phone: (502) 564-7962 Fax: (502) 564-9350
    Website: http://chfs.ky.gov/oig/drcc.htm
    Requirements: http://www.kdheks.gov/bcclr/lic_and_reg.html

- **Starting a day care in Louisiana**

    o Louisiana Department of Social Services
    Executive Office of the Secretary
    Bureau of Licensing
    2751 Wooddele Blvd.
    P.O. Box 3078
    Baton Rouge, LA 70821
    Phone: 225-922-0015
    Fax: 225-922-0014
    Website: http://www.ss.sdtate.la.us/departments/os/Licensing_.html
    Requirements: http://www.dss.state.la.us/departments/os/Licensing_.html#HowandWhere

- **Starting a day care in Maine**

    o Child Care Licensing
    Maine Department of Health and Human Services
    Marquardt Building 11 State House Station

Augusta, Maine 04333-0011
Phone: 207-287-5099
Fax: 207-287-5031
WebSite:
http://www.maine.gov/dhhs/ocfs/ec/occhs/infoparents.htm
Requirements:
http://www.maine.gov/dhhs/ocfs/ec/occhs/cclicensing.htm

- **Starting a day care in Maryland**

    - Maryland Department of Human Resources
      Child Care Administration
      311 W. Saratoga Street, 1st Floor
      Baltimore, MD 21201
      Phone: 410-767-7805
      Hotline: 800-332-6347
      Fax: 410-333-8699
      Website: http://mdchildcare.org/mdcfc/for_providers/TECHNIC.html
      Requirements: http://mdchildcare.org/mdcfc/for_providers/regulations.html

- **Starting a day care in Massachusetts**

    - Massachusetts Office of Child Care Services
      600 Washington Street, Suite 6100
      Boston, MA 02111
      Phone: 617-988-6600
      Fax: 617-988-2451
      Website:
      http://www.eec.state.ma.us/oo_licensing.aspx
      Requirements:
      http://www.eec.state.ma.us/oo_licensing.aspx

- **Starting a day care in Michigan**

    - Child Day Care Licensing
      Family Independence Agency
      Office of Children and Adult Licensing

7109 W. Saginaw, 2nd Floor
P.O. Box 30650
Lansing, MI 48909-8150
Phone: 517-335-6124 or 866-685-0006
Fax: 517-335-6121
Website: Starting a Day care in Michigan
Requirements: Michigan Licensing Requirements for Starting a Day care

- **Starting a day care in Minnesota**

    - Department of Human Services
    Division of Licensing
    444 Lafayette Road North
    St. Paul, MN 55155-3842
    Phone: 651-296-3971
    Fax: 651-297-1490
    Website: MN Dept of Human Services: Child Care
    Requirements: Minnesota Dept of Human Services: Child care Licensing

- **Starting a day care in Mississippi**

    - Child Care Facilities Licensure
    Mississippi State Department
    570 East Woodrow Wilson Drive
    P.O. Box 1700
    Jackson, MS 39215-1700
    Phone: 601-576-7613 or 800-227-7308
    Fax: 601-576-7813
    Website:
    http://www.msdh.state.ms.us/msdhsite/_static/41,0,81.html
    Requirements:
    http://www.msdh.state.ms.us/msdhsite/_static/30,0,183,225.html

- **Starting a day care in Missouri**

    - Missouri Department of Health and Senior Services

Bureau of Child Care
1715 Southridge Drive
P.O. Box 570
Jefferson City, MO 65109
Phone: 573-751-2891
Fax: 573-526-5345
Website: http://www.dss.mo.gov/pr_cs.htm
Requirements: http://www.dhss.mo.gov/Child care/LawsRegs.htm

- **Starting a day care in Montana**

    o Department of Public Health and Human Services (DPHHS)
    Quality Assurance Division (QAD) Licensing Bureau
    Child Care Licensing Program
    2401 Colonial Drive
    PO Box 202953
    Helena, MT 59620-2953
    Phone: 406-444-2012 or 406-444-7770
    Fax: 406-444-1742
    Website: Starting a Day care in Montana
    Requirements: Licensing Requirements for Starting a Day care in Montana

- **Starting a day care in Nebraska**

    o NE Department of Regulation and Licensure
    Credentialing Division Child Care
    P.O. Box 94986
    Lincoln, NE 68509-5044
    Phone: 402-471-9278 or 800-600-1289
    Fax: 402-471-7763
    Website: http://www.hhs.state.ne.us/chc/chcindex.htm
    Requirements: http://www.hhs.state.ne.us/crl/child care/child careindex.htm

- **Starting a day care in Nevada**

    - Department of Human Resources
      Division of Child and Family Services
      Bureau of Services for Child Care
      711 East 5th St. Carson, NV 89701
      Phone: 775-684-4463
      Hotline: 800-992-0900 (not in Elko or Las Vegas)
      Fax: 775-684-4464
      Website: http://www.dcfs.state.nv.us/page23.html
      Requirements:
      http://www.dcfs.state.nv.us/page23.html

- **Starting a day care in New Hampshire**

    - NH Dept. of Health and Human Services
      Office of Program Support
      Bureau of Child Care Licensing
      129 Pleasant Street
      Concord, NH 03301
      Phone: 603-271-4624
      Fax: 603-271-4782
      Website: http://www.dhhs.state.nh.us/dhhs/bccl
      Requirements:
      http://www.gencourt.state.nh.us/rules/he-c4000.html

- **Starting a ay care in New Jersey**

    - refers Family Child Care calls to counties

    - New Jersey Department of Human Services
      Office of Licensing
      Quakerbridge Plaza, Building 6
      P.O. Box 717
      Trenton, NJ 08625-0717
      Phone: 609-292-1018
      Fax: 609-292-6976
      Hotline: 877-667-9845
      Website:

http://www.state.nj.us/humanservices/dyfs/licensing.html
Requirements:
http://www.state.nj.us/dcf/divisions/licensing/laws.html

- **Starting a day care in New Mexico**

    o New Mexico Dept. of Children, Youth and Families
       Child Services Unit / Licensing
       1920 Fifth Street
       P.O. Drawer 5160
       Santa Fe, NM 87502-5160
       Fax: 505-827-7946
       Hotline: 800-610-7610 ext. 77499
       Website: http://www.newmexicokids.org/caregivers/
       Requirements:
       http://www.newmexicokids.org/caregivers/?view=/Resource/Regs/index.cfm#NewProposedRegulationChanges

- **Starting a day care in New York**

    o NY State Department of Family Assistance
       Office of Children and Family Services
       Bureau of Early Childhood Services
       52 Washington Street, Room 338, North Building
       Rensselaer, NY 12144
       Phone: 518-474-9454
       Fax: 518-474-9617
       Website: http://www.ocfs.state.ny.us/main/becs/
       Requirements:
       http://www.ocfs.state.ny.us/main/becs/day care_regs.asp

- **Starting a day care in North Carolina**

    o Division of Child Development Regulatory Services
       Section 319 Chapanoke Road, Suite 1202201
       Mail Service Center 27699-2201
       Raleigh, NC 27603

Phone: 919-662-4499 or 800-859-0829 (in-state calls only)
Fax: 919-661-4845
Website: http://ncchildcare.dhhs.state.nc.us/providers/pv_sn2_rcc.asp
Requirements: http://ncchildcare.dhhs.state.nc.us/providers/pv_sn2_lr.asp

- **Starting a day care in North Dakota**

    o Department of Human Services Early Childhood Services
    600 East Boulevard State Capitol Building
    Bismarck, ND 58505-0250
    Phone: 701-328-4809
    Fax: 701-328-3538
    Website: http://www.nd.gov/humanservices/services/childcare/
    Requirements http://www.nd.gov/humanservices/services/childcare/info/

- **Starting a day care in Ohio**

    o Ohio Department of Job & Family Services
    Bureau of Child Care and Development
    255 East Main Street, 3rd Floor
    Columbus, OH 43215-5222
    Phone: 614-466-1043
    Fax: 614-466-0164 or 614-728-6803
    Website: http://jfs.ohio.gov/cdc/general.stm#CCRP
    Requirements: http://jfs.ohio.gov/cdc/general.stm#CCRP

- **Starting a day care in Oklahoma**

    Department of Human Services Division of Child Care
    Sequoyah Memorial Office Building
    P.O. Box 25352
    Oklahoma City, OK 73125-0352
    Phone: 405-521-3561

Tollfree: 800-347-2276
Fax: 405-522-2564
Website: http://www.okdhs.org/programsandservices/cc/
Requirements: http://www.okdhs.org/programsandservices/cc/lic/docs/licensing.htm

- **Starting a day care in Oregon**

    - Oregon Department of Employment
    Child Care Division
    875 Union Street, NE
    Salem, OR 97311
    Phone: 503-947-1400
    Fax: 503-947-1428
    Website: http://findit.emp.state.or.us/child_care/
    Requirements: http://www.okdhs.org/programsandservices/cc/lic/

- **Starting a day care in Pennsylvania**

    - Pennsylvania Department of Public Welfare
    Bureau of Child Day Care
    Office of Children, Youth and Families Health and Welfare Building
    Room 131 P.O. Box 2675
    Harrisburg, PA 17105-2675
    Phone: 717-787-8691
    Fax: 717-787-1529
    Hotline: 877-4-PA-KIDS (within state)
    Website: http://www.dpw.state.pa.us/Child/Childcare/003671396.aspx
    Requirements: http://www.dpw.state.pa.us/Child/Childcare/003670452.htm

- **Starting a day care in Rhode Island**

    - Rhode Island Department of Children, Youth, and Families

Day Care Licensing Unit
101 Friendship Street
Providence, RI 02903
Phone: 401-528-3624 or 401-528-3621
Fax: 401-528-3650
Website: http://www.dcyf.ri.gov/day_care.php
Requirements: http://www.dcyf.ri.gov/licensing.php

- **Starting a day care in South Carolina**

    o Department of Social Services
    Division of Child Day Care Licensing and
    Regulatory Services
    2638 Two Notch Road, Suite 200
    Columbia, SC 29204
    Phone: 803-253-4049
    Fax: 803-252-1364
    Website: http://www.state.sc.us/dss/cdclrs/
    Requirements:
    http://www.state.sc.us/dss/cdclrs/overview.html

- **Starting a day care in South Dakota**

    o Department of Social Services Child Care Services
    Kneip Building 700 Governors Drive
    Pierre, SD 57501-2291
    Phone: 605-773-4766
    Fax: 605-773-7294
    Website: http://dss.sd.gov/child_care/
    Requirements: http://dss.sd.gov/child_care/licensing/

- **Starting a day care in Tennessee**

    o Tennessee Department of Human Services
    State Director Child & Adult Care Services
    Citizens Plaza Bldg. - 14th Floor
    400 Deaderick Street
    Nashville, TN 37248-9800
    Phone: 615-313-4770

Fax: 615-532-9956
Website:
http://www.state.tn.us/humanserv/adfam/cc_main.htm
Requirements:
http://www.state.tn.us/sos/rules/1240/1240-04/1240-04.htm

- **Starting a day care in Texas**

    o Department of Family and Protective Services
    Child Care Licensing
    P.O. Box 149030701 W. 51st Street
    Austin, TX 78714-9030
    Phone: 512-438-4800
    Hotline: 800-862-5252
    Fax: 512-438-3848
    Website:
    http://www.dfps.state.tx.us/Child_Care/Search_Texas_Child_Care/
    Requirements:
    http://www.dfps.state.tx.us/Child_Care/About_Child_Care_Licensing/

- **Starting a day care in Utah**

    o Department of Health
    Office of Child Care Licensing
    P.O. Box 142003
    Salt Lake City, UT 84114-2003
    Phone: 801-538-6152
    Fax: 801-538-9259
    Website: http://www.health.utah.gov/licensing/ChildcareInfo.htm
    Requirements : http://www.health.utah.gov/licensing

- **Starting a day care in Vermont**

    o Department for Children and Families
    Child Developmental Division
    Child Care Licensing Unit103 South. Main

Street, 2 North
Waterbury, VT 05671-2901
Phone: 802-241-3110
Fax: 802-241-1220
Website: http://www.dcf.state.vt.us/cdd/programs/childcare/index.html
Requirements:
http://www.dcf.state.vt.us/cdd/programs/childcare/licensing.html

- **Starting a day care in Virginia**

    o Virginia Department of Social Services
    Division of Licensing Programs
    7 North Eighth Street
    Richmond, VA 23219
    Phone: 800-543-7545 (within state) or 804-662-9743 (nationwide)
    Fax: 804-662-9743
    Website: http://www.dss.virginia.gov/family/cc/business.cgi
    Requirements: Licensing Requirements for Starting a Day care in Virginia

- **Starting a day care in Washington**

    o Washington Department of Social and Health Services
    Economic Services Administration Division of Child Care and Early Learning
    P.O. Box 45480
    Olympia, WA 98504-5480
    Phone: 360-725-4665
    Fax: 360-413-3482
    Hotline: 866-482-4325
    Website: http://www.del.wa.gov/ccel/index.shtml
    Requirements:
    http://www.del.wa.gov/ccel/faq.shtml#cclq1b

- **Starting a day care in West Virginia**

    o   West Virginia Department of Health and Human Resources
        Bureau for Children and Families Office of Children and Family Policy
        Division of Early Care and Education
        350 Capitol Street, B18
        Charleston, WV 25301-3700
        Website:
        http://www.wvdhhr.org/bcf/ece/earlycare/startcenter.asp

        Family Child Care
        Phone: 304-558-1885
        Fax: 304-558-8800
        Requirements:
        http://www.wvdhhr.org/bcf/ece/earlycare/startcenter.asp

- **Starting a day care in Wisconsin**

    o   Division of Children & Family Services
        Bureau of Regulation and Licensing
        1 West Wilson Street Room 534
        P.O. Box 8916
        Madison, WI 53708-8916
        Phone: 608-266-9314
        Fax: 608-267-7252
        Website: http://dcf.wisconsin.gov/child care/licensed/Starting.HTM
        Requirements: http://dcf.wisconsin.gov/child care/licensed/Rules.HTM

- **Starting a day care in Wyoming**

    o   Department of Family Services
        Division of Early Childhood
        2300 Capitol Avenue Hathaway Building, 3rd Floor
        Cheyenne, WY 82002-0490
        Phone: 307-777-5491
        Fax: 307-777-3659

Website:
http://dfswapps.state.wy.us/DFSDivEC/Providers/ProvidersPCC.asp Requirements:
http://dfswapps.state.wy.us/DFSDivEC/General/LicensingRules.asp

- **Starting a day care in Puerto Rico**

    o Department of Family
    Licensing Office
    P.O. Box 11398
    Santurce, PR 00910
    Phone: 787-724-0772
    Fax: 787-724-0767
    Website:
    http://nrc.uchsc.edu/STATES/PR/puertorico.htm

- **Starting a day care in Virgin Islands**

    o Department of Human Services
    Child Care Licensing
    3011 Golden Rock
    Christiansted, St. Croix
    U.S. Virgin Islands 00820-4355
    Phone: 340-773-2323
    Fax: 340-773-6121
    Website:
    http://nrc.uchsc.edu/STATES/VI/virginislands.htm

ACTIVITIES

Planning a curriculum is one of the most important duties. Developing curriculum requires an expert, particularly for the older children. Curriculum will be more intensive, of course, as children get older, but a planned schedule is needed even for the younger children. In general, play time will occur in the morning, from arrival time until around 9:00. Then, the first learning session should occur, which will last for about an hour and a half. This session may include several different activities focused on a central theme. Next, may come a morning snack and then a play session until lunch.

Story time and napping should occur after lunch. Following that, another learning session, another snack time and another time allocated for play should occur. The schedule should include plenty of physical activity for the children.

It may be helpful to work with the Chamber of Commerce, civic clubs, and city administration to enhance the children's schedule. Children love visits by policemen, firemen and others who talk to them about citizenship and roles in the community.

Student teachers, artists and other upper classmen at local colleges should be invited to visit and work with the kids on drawing, building, origami and many other things. It is important to bring outsiders in to talk to the kids about what happens in their world.

Bringing in outside companies for some of the activities is helpful, particularly if school age children are coming for after school care.

Some of the activities to consider include:

- Music

- Gymnastics

- Computer Classes – some companies will come in and teach computer skills to children as young as age 2.

- Martial Arts

- Dance

- Foreign Language Classes

These classes will, of course, charge for their services. However, parents will usually be glad to have access to these programs for their children, and many will sign up if they are offered. Parents can pay the outside companies directly if they choose to sign their children up, or a deal may be made between the day care and the companies that can be financially beneficial. If a certain number of children sign up for their programs, the company will charge a lower rate per student. The day care center can collect the fees and charge the regular rate to parents. This allows for a profit to be made for the use of the facility for the classes.

INSURANCE

Insurance is critical for the business and also required by law in most states. The day care center is responsible, or liable in insurance terms, for these children when they are in day care. Unfortunately, accidents can and do happen, leaving the day care open to exposure. For example, parents could sue for negligence if their child is injured while at the day care. If the center was found guilty and had no insurance, it would have to pay the child's family out of pocket.

Liability insurance protects the day care center from such incidents. When purchasing liability insurance for the day care, the center will be protected up to the limits of the policy purchased. The policy limit is the maximum amount the insurance company will pay for covered claims.

There are two important reasons to buy liability coverage. Of course, the center wants the protection of knowing the center is insured and financially protected. But, it is also comforting to know that the center has the insurance company on its side and its expertise to defend the center in court in the event of a suit.

Finally, the insurance company can often help to prevent accidents and claims. Most companies who offer liability insurance will also provide consulting to help ensure that the facility is safe and less likely to be the site of an accident. This keeps overall costs down and children safe.

CHOOSING AN INSURANCE COMPANY

It is important to shop around before choosing an insurance carrier.

Consider the following when interviewing insurance companies.

- It should have An A.M. Best rating of "A" or higher (A.M. Best rates insurance companies on the basis of their financial strength and ability to pay claims.)

- It should be a company that writes a lot of child care business or has a special program for the industry.

- It should be a company that has a solid loss control and risk management program to help maintain a safe environment.

Every question imaginable should be asked to ensure the coverage is fully explained and understood. Like many other things, cheaper insurance may not be better insurance. It is important to balance afforadble cost with adequate coverage. It should be remembered that liability insurance premiums are tax deductible. It is extrememly important the day care center has the propoer coverage in order to avoid disaster.

5
MARKETING

Regardless of how great a day care program may be, it is worthless unless the public is aware the business exists. In time, word of mouth advertising will works wonders, but aggressive marketing needs to occur to bring the children in the door.

Here are some of the best tools for marketing to potential customers:

THE SIGN

A sign is one of the best advertisements. It is amazing how many people will investigate the services simply because they drove by and liked the signage. Check with the licensing office if it is acceptable to post a sign in a residential yard. If it is permitted, one should work with a professional sign company to create a very professional, permanent sign for the facility. The more information provided on the sign about the services, the better the response will be. Of course, the phone numbers and hours of operation should be easily readable, and the sign should be designed in fun and vibrant colors.

BROCHURE

A professional printing company should be hired to produce brochures about the business. Credentials, basic business information, services provided, a picture of the facility, and contact information should be included. Pricing is subject to change, so it should not be included in the brochure in order to avoid reprinting as pricing changes occur. These brochures should be handed out each time a potential client gets a tour. It is also effective to find other local businesses that will allow you to leave your brochures in their stores or offices. Pediatric offices, children's clothing stores and any other business parents frequent are good choices. If after school care is being offered, the principals of the local elementary schools should be introduced to your facility so they also can refer potential clients.

GRAND OPENING OPEN HOUSE

A big grand opening event is a great way to introduce the business. An event takes a lot of planning and it is crucial the public is aware of the event to ensure high attendance. Advertising with banners, newspaper ads, and local radio ads are great ways to spread the word. There should be entertainment for the children, as well as drinks and snacks for the entire crowd. In many cases, particularly where there's a real need for day care in the area, a center can nearly complete maximum enrollment through a good open house.

In the weeks before the open house, as remodeling nears completion, start keeping regular business hours, and put the opening date on the sign. During these weeks, there should be plenty of parents dropping in to check out the facility and ask questions. Some parents may enroll their children during these visits. In addition, the business phone should be working as soon as possible and answered during business hours to provide information to potential clients.

LOCAL MEDIA

Local media is one of the most effective ways to advertise the day care. Local newspapers, business listings, and nearby neighbor newspapers should be utilized to let the public know the day care is opening.

6
CUSTOMER SERVICE

Once the doors are open, providing excellent customer service is a top priority. One of the best ways to get off to a good start with parents and children is to make expectations clear from the start. Confusion and misunderstandings often arise when rules and expectations aren't made clear to everyone at the onset. Set up and design a Parent Manual to provide to parents at the time of enrollment so they may see the rules and regulations in writing. Give them time to discuss any items that they may have a question about after reviewing the Parent Manual.

The Parent Manual should answer some of these pertinent questions below:

1. **Who provides formula and diapers for infants?** In most day cares, parents provide formula, results are split about diapers, with some day cares providing them and others requiring parents to bring them.

2. **Are children allowed to bring toys from home?** In most cases, the answer is no, because the day care does not want to be responsible if a child's favorite toy goes missing. Though, many day cares do allow the children to bring a blanket for sleeping. If plenty of good age-specific toys are provided at the center, children should adapt quickly to having toys for home and toys at school.

3. **When is payment expected?**
   Most day cares expect payment for the week on Friday morning, with a late fee assessed on Monday morning. It is best to charge ahead of schedule to assure payment for that enrollment is made on time.

4. **Is outside food allowed?**
   If children with special dietary requirements are enrolled, it may be beneificla to allow parents to bring in food for their children. Outside of food allergies or other dietary needs, it is not wise to allow kids to bring in food from home.

5. **How to handle late pickups?**
   It is inevitable that sometimes parents will not make the pickup deadline. This is often due to circumstances beyond their control, and the day care needs to be understanding. However, the center may also have some chronic offenders. It is wise to make a policy of charging a fee for late pickups. It should be costly enough to discourage parents who simply are not trying hard enough to be there on time. Many day cares charge $5 per minute late and give the money directly to the staff member who has to stay late with the child.

Holidays and vacations
The holiday schedule should be posted for an entire year in advance. The center should be closed on normal holidays, such as Thanksgiving Day and Christmas Day. Be clear on payment for absences and holidays in your Parent Manual.

Even when expectations are clear, issues will arise. The director should take care of issues quickly and in a manner that is fair to all parties. Often parents will complain about activities in the classroom or be unhappy with a teacher's decision.

The staff members should clearly know the rules they are expected to follow, and should alert the director immediately when something goes awry in the classroom.

When making decisions, it is always important to handle situations fairly. Parents pay tuition and have a right to feel comfortable about the care their children are receiving. On the other hand, the teachers need to know they are supported. It is often wise to settle disputes between parents and staff by sitting down with them to discuss the situation. Do not allow the children to be involved in these discussions.

One of the most important things to keep parents happy with the facility, outside of keeping it running smoothly, keeping it clean and keeping the programs fresh and staffing consistent, is for the director to always be there.

The director job requires "management by walking around." The director needs to know the students and parents by name and needs to be there when they come in to pick up their kids. Only when the director and the staff become like family will the center be able to weather any issues with families as they arise. The director must always be professional, of course, but remember that when working with children, closeness and a hands on approach are the most successful.

7
BEING PROFITABLE

Unless the business is a nonprofit agency, it is there to make money and there is money to be made in the day care business because the need is always present. But, there are many upfront costs, and many ongoing expenses for which to plan.

These are some upfront expenses to plan for during remodeling or set up of the facility.

UPFRONT EXPENSES

> Licensing Fees
> Advertising
> First Aid/CPR Certification
> Liability Insurance
> High Chairs
> Booster Seats
> Nap Mats (these could also be charged to each family as part of an initial registration fee)
> Playpens/Portable Cribs
> Bedding
> Smoke detectors and fire alarms
> First Aid Kit
> Computers
> Locks and safety equipment for doors
> Books
> Toys
> Educational Materials
> Arts & Crafts Supplies

Disposable Gloves
Disposable Changing Pads
Antibacterial Cleaners
Food
Child-sized Tables and Chairs
Sanitary Storage for Used Diapers
Step Stools for Sink and Toilet
Outdoor Play Space (swings and playground, balls, etc.)
Make-believe Props, Clothes and Costumes for Dressing Up
CD Player and CDs of children's music
Kitchen Supplies – pots and pans, dishes, etc.

ONGOING EXPENSES

The biggest ongoing expense is the compensation paid to the assistants. Competitive wages should be offered and accounted for in the business plan. One must determine the number of children to serve, which will determine the amount of staff required. Hire less experienced individuals to act as teaching assistants, helping out in the classrooms under the direction of the lead teacher. Remember that the law dictates the number of teachers required based on the number of students in the classroom. These assistants will be paid less and some may work on a part time basis.

The costs of meal preparation and cleaning supplies for your facility need also be budgeted. Another of the larger ongoing costs is for food. However, this is also an area where one can save money by shopping wisely. Be certain to spend an appropriate amount of time learning how to get the best deals on food.

Other ongoing costs are supplies, art and teaching materials, as well as monthly bills for rent and utilities. A loan payment may also be a monthly expense. The wages should be set to reflect the going rates at other day cares, and some part time employees may be paid just minimum wage. To be able to attract and keep the best employees, one needs to consider offering benefits, like medical insurance, paid vacation and paid sick leave. Each employee's salary must reflected in the budget The salary budget must be completed before tuition rates are determined.

TUITION RATES

Once the operating costs are known, it is time to calculate the tuition rates. It is critical that the rates are competitive with other day cares in the area.

If the rates are going to be significantly higher than others in the area, this difference must be justified. If the food is more nutritionally sound because a nutritionist designed the menu, advertise this point. Anything that sets the center apart wins points with parents and helps justify higher tuition.

To keep things simple, it might be wise to structure the tuition rates the same way other day cares do, so that it is easy to compare apples to apples. For example, if other centers do not include the price of breakfast as part of their tuition, but charge it as an add-on instead, it might be wise to do the same.

When most parents are shopping for a day care, cost is not the number one deciding factor. The most important factor to parents is the feeling that their children will be well taken care of in the facility.

Profitability is a delicate balance of managing costs and charging appropriately. But, it is really important to create this balance before the doors ever open.

SETTING THE DAY CARE APART

It is a good idea, from a profitability perspective, to create an identity for the day care. This helps with marketing, hiring employees and setting prices. As mentioned earlier, the center can charge more if it can show how it is delivering more value to the customer.

There are quite a few ways to create this difference. Adding value through extra programs is the best way. Some day cares pride themselves on being a program dedicated to the arts, while others offer large libraries and work hard on reading programs. Many day cares have also created quite an advantage through their food programs (such as removing processed foods from their menus) or by offering unusual hours, therefore catering to a specific market of parent.

8
WHY DAY CARES FAIL

Most day care centers can rely on maintaining a reasonable enrollment once they are established. In fact, statistics show that most day cares reach 90% capacity within six months of opening their doors. In areas where there is a real shortage of day care, centers can reach these enrollment rates within six weeks. So, if there is such a great need for day cares, why do some fail?

These are the top reasons for failure:

FINANCIAL FAILURE

As mentioned earlier, the balance between managing costs and creating income is a delicate one, and is the balance day care centers have the most trouble with. Tuitions that are too low, parents who don't pay and costs that are too high can put a day care in the red very quickly. For this reason, it is critical that the budget is balanced. All costs need be accounted for, including preparing for increases that could happen to those costs. Though the tuition rates must be competitive, they must also be high enough to cover costs. Understand that, above and beyond the salary the owner takes, the center may not make any real profits for a few years, particularly until loans used for startup costs are paid off. Make sure any investors understand this before investing.

FAILURE TO ADHERE TO LEGAL GUIDELINES

It is critical that one understands that the day care can be shut down if it fails to adhere to state regulations. This includes not having enough staff on site at all times.

Many day cares combine classes early in the morning and late in the afternoon in order to cut staffing costs. This strategy works, as long as the student to staff ratio required by law is followed. Parents will report the center if they see an infraction and an investigation may follow. In addition, licensing agencies may show up for visits, and will cite the center for violations. It is critical to know the laws and constantly adhere to them.

FAILURE TO SATISFY CUSTOMERS

If parents are unhappy with the day care center, word will spread rapidly. Keeping customers happy requires the following items.

Many of these have been mentioned earlier, but they are so critical they bear repeating:

- Maintain a consistent staff, who are appropriately educated, reliable, competent and caring.

- Keep a clean and safe facility.

- Serve nutritious food for meals and snacks.

- Adhere to all regulations.

- Provide appropriate educational experiences that grow with the children.

- Provide plenty of physical activities and stimulation.
- Set rules and communicate them clearly.
- Maintain open communication with parents and staff. Resolve disputes quickly and fairly.
- Be available to the students and parents; get to know them and listen to their concerns.
- Be willing to make changes as necessary to keep the program thriving.
- Stay on top of trends in the industry. When other day cares make changes, be willing to follow suit if they make sense for the business.
- Provide a good working environment for the staff. A staff that is happy with its work environment will do a better job than an unhappy staff. Also, provide ongoing training for the staff to keep them current in their credentials and to give them more education in the field.

Making and keeping a day care successful and profitable is a constant job. The owner needs to stay on top of all the aspects of the business to keep it legal and to keep the customers happy. This constant attention to the needs of the students and the business is what will keep the business thriving.

9
CREATING A LONG TERM PLAN

Once the day care is up and running and has achieved a good enrollment number, the owner can breathe a sigh of relief. If the budget is working and it is verified that there is enough money coming in to meet expenses and pay salaries, then the center is in good shape. The first step is therefore completed successfully.

But, it is important to understand that in order to remain successful, one needs to constantly evolve and make long-term plans.

The following areas will always need attention:

- **Staffing**
  Staff will leave, and occasionally a staff member will need to be fired. There may also be times when additional staff need to hired, such as when enrollment increases and the center provides full time care to elementary age children during the summer months.

- **Marketing**
  Even if the facility is full at the moment, there will be times when there will be openings that need filling. Children will age out of the program and families will move. The day care owner needs to keep various marketing avenues open, and find

ways to keep the costs of marketing minimal when the center is full.

- **Licensing**
  The day care will have to be relicensed periodically by the state, and the kitchen will also be inspected by the health department periodically. If keeping the day care up to standard is simply part of the daily routine, these times will not be a problem. But, if the facility is allowed to slip, re-licensing or inspections may be difficult. There may also be times when regulations change, and these changes must be made to the facility to adhere to new rules.

- **Curriculum**
  Day care curriculum should be evaluated periodiclaly. As new trends emerge and new learning technologies become available, parents expect the curriculum to keep up. In some cases, keeping the curriculum fresh is simply a matter of keeping current with the community. If a new museum opens up, take the students on a field trip. If the trip is successful, this trip should be added to the yearly curriculum of the age group it suits best.

- **Expansion**
  If the day care started small, expansion plans should be considered. A larger facility may be needed in the future or classroom density may be increased. These enhancements can help the program attract more students, but all enhancements require planning and capital. By keeping expansion ideas in mind, one can budget for them to make them happen when the facility is ready.

  In some cases, expansion may not be anything as ambitious as adding on to the facility, but can include expanding the programs offered. Adding a music program or bringing in outside companies to offer dance and other programs may have been too ambitious to offer opening day, but may be a great thing to add in the future. Even simple ideas like working with a publishing company to offer a yearly book fair are great ways to make long term plans.

- **Communication**
  Once the business is up and running, some in-house communication vehicles for the day care center should be considered. A newsletter that goes home to parents each week is a good idea, and will keep the parents feeling informed and connected. Another great communication vehicle is a bulletin board in the lobby. Postings can include announcements, and can can even feature one class each month, by posting the children's pictures and artwork. Parents are thrilled when their kids are in the spotlight.

CONCLUSION

Owning and running a day care can be a very rewarding and financially lucrative experience. If the day care center does an outstanding job, parents and children will be forever grateful and will always remember the experiences they had at the facility. For the day care owner/operator who loves kids, nothing could be more rewarding.

The day care business is one that has great potential and will continue to be in high demand. Starting a day care center is quite a challenge, but it can also be just the opportunity to create one's own business, doing what one loves and earn a satisfying income. Hopefully, the tips provided here will put any potential day care owner well on the way to creating a business to be proud of.

ABOUT THE AUTHOR

Kriston Gordon-Cathey, M.ED. is on a mission to honor children and empower parents around the world with proven, road-tested, and simple parenting strategies that reduce struggles and add more joy for every member of the family.

While operating a successful child care business for over 10 years, Kriston is nicknamed "the child whisperer" by many happy families who value her gift to see each child's perspective as they use her methods to bring harmony to their formerly conflicted families. She teaches parenting workshops and shares keynote presentations to parenting groups that put prevention strategies on center stage.

Kriston Cathey grew up in Los Angeles, California, earned a Bachelor of Arts degree in Communications, Masters in Education and is currently a candidate for her Doctorate in Education. She resides in Maryland with her husband and two children.

Made in the USA
Lexington, KY
29 July 2018